Bible Study

7 Sessions for Homegroup and Personal Use

GW00393969

Isaiah 1-39

Prophet to the nations

John Houghton

Copyright © CWR, 2009

Published 2009 by CWR, Waverley Abbey House, Waverley Lane, Farnham, Surrey GU9 8EP, UK. Registered Charity No. 294387. Registered Limited Company No. 1990308.

The right of John Houghton to be identified as the author of this work has been asserted by him in accordance with the Copyright, Designs and Patents Act 1988, sections 77 and 78.

See back of book for list of National Distributors.

Unless otherwise indicated, all Scripture references are from the Holy Bible: New International Version (NIV), copyright © 1973, 1978, 1984 by the International Bible Society.

Concept development, editing, design and production by CWR
Cover image: iStockphoto/Pixcel Animation

Printed in Latvia by Yeomans Press

ISBN: 978-1-85345-510-0

Contents

Introduction

Isaiah was an educated man from a noble family and
enjoyed close contact with the royal court. His wife
was a prophetess and they had at least two sons. A
contemporary with the prophets Hosea and Micah, he
prophesied in Jerusalem from c.740–680BC, covering the
reigns of the Judaean kings, Uzziah, Jotham, Ahaz and
Hezekiah.

The united kingdoms of Judah in the south, and Israel
in the north, had split back in 931 BC during the time of
King Solomon's successor, Rehoboam. The separation had
left a legacy of political tension and sporadic civil war.
When Isaiah started prophesying, morally and politically,
the northern kingdom was falling apart. With its disastrous
idolatry and social injustice, it had only eighteen years left
before it would be obliterated for ever by the Assyrians. The
southern kingdom was in danger of going the same way.

The Assyrian power, situated in Mesopotamia, west of the
Zagros mountains and north of the Chaldean kingdom,
had its capital in Nineveh. Its imperial expansion would
last from 750–612 BC. Less geographically protected from
eastern mountain raiders than the Chaldeans in the south,
it embarked on a military expansion to secure its territory
and protect its vital trade routes. Having subdued the
east, under its vigorous king, Tiglath-Pileser III (745–727
BC), Assyria began to expand its empire westwards,
conquering all the small nations, including Israel and most
of Judah. Samaria, the capital of Israel, fell in 722 BC and
Jerusalem looked set to be next.

Isaiah foresaw, in spite of evidence to the contrary,
that the main judgment on Judah would not come from
Assyria but from a resurgent Babylon, some one hundred
years later. This has led some to challenge the unity of

the book, suggesting two, perhaps even three, authors of Isaiah. However, there is no compelling reason to do so unless we wish to deny the possibility of predictive prophecy. We have split the book in two simply because of its sheer size and because the break marks a logical transition in subject matter.

The military advance of the Assyrians was seen by Isaiah as the judgment of God. Indeed, God describes Assyria as no less than 'the rod of my anger, in whose hand is the club of my wrath!' (Isa. 10:5). The great sins that brought judgment on Israel, and later Judah, were moral decadence, political corruption, social injustice and spiritual idolatry. All this was masked by outward religious observance. Isaiah's calling was to expose the hypocrisy, but he was promised little success in his lifetime. Prophets are by definition outsiders, heretics, a threat to the establishment, killjoys. All he could hope for was a faithful remnant. Yet, one day from this band of pilgrims would emerge the Anointed One, the Messiah, who would establish His government over the whole world. Even the Gentile nations would come to worship Him – an amazing prediction anticipating the new covenant where there would be 'neither Jew nor Greek, slave nor free, male nor female, for you are all one in Christ Jesus' (Gal. 3:28). We are seeing this prophecy fulfilled today in the global spread of the gospel.

Isaiah is the Messianic prophet above all others. Often compressing time, and also telescoping immediate prophecies into the distant future, he predicts both Christ's first and second advents. Their remarkable fulfilment in the life of Jesus of Nazareth assures us that the word will prove to be just as reliable when Jesus returns in glory.

Isaiah's message of holiness challenges us personally but it is addressed nationally. Although we cannot simply equate the unique status of God's Old Testament people with, say, the United Kingdom, or with the national Church, nonetheless, we are an apostolically evangelised nation and it is perfectly legitimate for us to call the nation and its Church back to God's ways. We may have no more success than Isaiah but we must still respond to the voice of the Lord saying, 'Whom shall I send? And who will go for us?' (Isa. 6:8).

Prophetic perspectives are covenant based. They call us back to our original commitment so that we may go forward, and when they are predictive it is not mere fortune-telling – the prophecies point us to the unfolding of the divine plan for our lives and to the fulfilment of God's covenant promises. Using powerful poetic imagery, the prophet disturbs our complacency and challenges our backsliding. He calls us to repentance and to change our behaviour so that we may re-engage with the redemptive journey that is our pilgrim calling. It is a call to inward separation from the vices of this passing age and a commitment to walk the highway of holiness, not as supercilious, 'holier-than-thou' prigs, but as those who are lovingly, mercifully and diligently engaged with everyday life and society. As Peter puts it: '... you are a chosen people, a royal priesthood, a holy nation, a people belonging to God, that you may declare the praises of Him who called you out of darkness into his wonderful light' (1 Pet. 2:9).

Finally, although we shall be able to cover the main themes of this great prophecy, we recommend that you read a chapter a day in order to gain the maximum benefit from the study.

WEEK 1

The National Disease

Opening Icebreaker

See how many direct connections you can make between sins and sicknesses and accidents. Remember that sometimes there is no immediate connection to be made, so don't make the infirm among you feel guilty for no good reason!

Bible Readings

Isaiah 1:1–31   ✳ Isaiah 53:4–6
Hosea 4:1–3   James 1:27
Isaiah 5:1–12

Key verse: 'Though your sins are like scarlet, they shall be as white as snow …' Isaiah 1:18

Focus: Religion is no substitute for true holiness.

Opening Our Eyes

God hates hypocrisy and Isaiah's perspective, as a true prophet, is one that exposes the shocking truth about our human condition. His words are unequivocal, calling heaven and earth to witness: God the Father has raised children who have become rebels. His own people have provoked the Holy One of Israel to anger and are suffering the consequences.

The nation is sick from head to toe. Morally and spiritually, it is an untreated putrefying mess. Divine judgment that should have brought about repentance has left the nation in economic ruin and its cities destroyed. Politically, Jerusalem is reduced to a hut in a field, isolated and alone.

Yet religious activity continues as though nothing were amiss. Offerings are given, sacrifices are made, festivals celebrated, prayers offered as if unrighteous behaviour didn't count, or sin could be offset by ritual observance. This is sheer hypocrisy. 'I am sick of it!' says the Lord. 'What is the point or value of religious ritual without a pure heart and a holy life? I never asked for this nonsense, so don't think it will cut any ice with me. I won't listen to your prayers until you reform your behaviour and cleanse yourselves from your sins!'

Top of the sin list is political, social and economic injustice. Laws favouring the rich had led to the deprivation of the poor and the appropriation of their land and property by the rich and powerful. Bribery and corruption had become endemic, with government and business people alike negotiating dishonest deals with rogues and gangsters. Widows and orphans were being swindled for the benefit of crooks. Good is called evil, and evil is called good.

A celebrity culture of self-centred hedonism with
an obsession for fashion and partying had created a
superficial consumer society indifferent to anything of real
value or importance. The cult of the body had replaced
the growth of the soul. Heroism was now measured by
the ability to mix and drink cocktails! Alcohol abuse had
become so endemic that even the priests and prophets
were slouched drunk in their own vomit.

If that were not enough, eastern occultism had infiltrated
the popular consciousness. Fortune-telling was rife and a
brisk trade in idols had polluted the pure worship of God.
Once-holy Jerusalem had become a brazen prostitute, as
vain and callous as Sodom and Gomorrah. God's chosen
people had made themselves His enemies.

The scene is set for further judgment. God is determined
to purify His people, for it is in them that His salvation
purpose for the whole world is invested. Although the
judgment will be severe, there will be survivors who will
heed the word of the Lord. From a faithful remnant will
one day come the Messiah, the Servant of the Lord, who
will offer Himself as the redemptive sacrifice for the sins
of the whole world. Zion will be redeemed and will be
renamed 'the City of Righteousness, the Faithful City',
surely a pointer to the New Jerusalem (Rev. 21:1–2).

Who constitutes this remnant? All those who respond to
a remarkable and gracious offer of divine mercy. The
Lord invites His people to the conference table and offers
them a deal. If they repent and reform their ways, their
sins, even though inflamed scarlet, can be made as white
as snow. Those who are willing to cleanse themselves
and re-educate themselves in goodness and truth will be
blessed. Those who don't will be destroyed by a fearful
war of judgment.

Discussion Starters

1. What parallels can you draw between the state of Isaiah's nation and that of our own today? What should we do about it?

2. Those who draw near to God must do so with clean hands and a pure heart (Psa. 24:3–4). What does this mean in practical terms?

3. Isaiah's perspective was not popular in his day, but it proved to be true. How do we expose sin and speak of the judgment of God without simply being obnoxious?

4. We are told to wash ourselves and to reform our ways. What steps would you take should you need to respond to this?

5. Jesus died to heal us from our sins and sicknesses. How would you share this good news with your friends, colleagues, family and neighbours?

_____

_____

_____

_____

6. Faithful remnants can easily become quirky groups and communities that have little connection with society. How can we live as God's holy people and yet still interact with the world around us?

_____

_____

_____

_____

7. Political, social and economic justice is high on God's agenda. How can we best engage in the political process to bring this about in our society and beyond?

_____

_____

_____

_____

Personal Application

It is all too easy to attend church, participate in the services, and yet be far from the Lord in our own hearts. This may be because of known sin, or it may be because our minds are distracted by the cares and vanities of this world, or we may simply have grown indifferent through force of habit. Isaiah issues us with a wake-up call. Consider your ways. Commit yourself afresh to a life dedicated to the Lord who gave His life for you. You belong among His faithful remnant – those who choose to pilgrim on the fresh-air highway of holiness rather than to wallow in the stinking swamps of sin. Be who you were called to be!

Seeing Jesus in the Scriptures

The most shocking truth in Scripture is that Christ, the Sinless One, became sin for us. Bearing the judgment of God on our behalf, He embodied on the cross all that is corrupt in human nature, so much so that Isaiah says '… his appearance was so disfigured beyond that of any man and his form marred beyond human likeness …' (Isa. 52:14). Murder, anger, lust, deceit, greed, pride – and every other sin; cancer, diabetes, skin diseases, heart disease, brain damage, plague – and every other sickness; all this fell on Jesus. These are our sins, our sicknesses: surely 'the Lord has laid on him the iniquity of us all', and 'by his wounds we are healed' (Isa. 53:5–6).

To ignore this is to reject our one hope of salvation. To accept it surely demands 'my soul, my life, my all' (Isaac Watts, 1674–1748).

WEEK 2

The Day of the Lord

Opening Icebreaker

Create a law court scenario with one member of the group assuming the role of judge. The other members are the prosecuting counsel bringing charges against the world. In turn, 'I charge the world with ...' How many different major crimes can you come up with?

Bible Readings

Isaiah 2:1–22   2 Peter 3:10–13
Isaiah 34:1–4   Revelation 21:1–5
Luke 21:23–28

Key verse: '"He will teach us his ways, so that we may walk in his paths." The law will go out from Zion ...'
Isaiah 2:3

Focus: The day of judgment will also be the day of redemption.

Opening Our Eyes

Christians are often suspicious of law. After all, through Christ we have been delivered from the curse of the law – and many of us know about the dangers of legalism, when duty becomes a substitute for true devotion. Grace and faith are our watchwords. Yet the Bible insists that we need law to govern society. The passage before us prophesies the global hope of universal peace when the law goes out from Zion under the Messiah's reign.

This is heralded by the day of the Lord, a day that commences with judgment on the ungodly, the unjust and the arrogant. The imminent judgment of Israel, Judah and Jerusalem becomes a metaphor for what will happen to the whole world: material and human resources will fail, government in the hands of the inept will collapse, fashionable culture will fall apart, the party is over, death will stalk the land, people will hide underground, the principalities and powers – both human and spiritual – will be judged, and the world will end. It's a sobering thought.

There are two observations to make. First, judgment is deserved. Our sophisticated modern world consistently denies the corruption of human nature and systems. It is a shock when we discover the evils of dictators, the genocides, the children forced to eat one another alive, the raping and torture, the millions killed under Stalin, Hitler, Mao Tsung and Pol Pot, the ruination of millions by bankers, the corruption of power. We would prefer not to see it. We blame anything but human nature. But God sees it all. 'The heart is deceitful above all things and beyond cure. Who can understand it? I the LORD search the heart and examine the mind, to reward a man according to his conduct, according to what his deeds deserve' (Jer. 17:9–10).

Given the lack of human justice in the world, particularly for the poor and vulnerable, we should be glad that a day is coming when the Judge of all the earth will do right, and no longer will there be a hiding place for corruption.

Second, this day of the Lord heralds the return of Christ, the bodily resurrection of the dead, the vindication of the saints, the reconciliation of all things, the end of sin, suffering and injustice, the inauguration of a new cosmos. Jesus said, speaking about the end of time, 'When these things begin to take place, stand up and lift up your heads, because your redemption is drawing near' (Luke 21:28).

Christian hope centres on the return of Christ and the resurrection from the dead. It is an event that should motivate and inspire us to live faithfully and passionately for our Lord. Isaiah anticipates the new Jerusalem where people of all nations have ended their warring and live in eternal peace. The lion will lie down with the lamb and the child will play happily with the snake. This is when God makes all things new, when all pain and sorrow and separation is ended and His glorious presence fills the world with light.

It is the pattern of all things, the life–death–resurrection waveform of creation and of redemption. The Son of God humbles Himself even to death and is raised to new life. We lose our lives in baptismal death to find ourselves anew in Christ. The world must end in judgment, but this death will usher in the new heavens and the new earth. Little wonder John ends our Bibles with the passionate cry, 'Amen. Come, Lord Jesus.'

Discussion Starters

1. Why do you think human beings long for justice?

_____
_____
_____
_____
_____

2. Is it still possible to believe in a God of wrath? If so, how do we communicate the idea?

_____
_____
_____
_____
_____

3. What do you think it means to say that Jesus bore the wrath of God on our behalf when He died on the cross?

_____
_____
_____
_____
_____

4. What assurance can you offer to those who fear that they are too bad and are beyond redemption?

_____
_____
_____
_____
_____

5. Some people expect the world to end quite soon. How would you express your Christian hope for the future?

_____

_____

_____

_____

_____

6. How can we best live our days in the light of Christ's second coming?

_____

_____

_____

_____

_____

7. When Jesus returns, what do you think the new heaven and earth will be like, 'the home of righteousness'?

_____

_____

_____

_____

_____

Personal Application

The apostle Peter reminds us that we cannot book the day of the Lord in our diaries. It will come suddenly, unexpectedly, in one cataclysmic moment. He urges us to live holy and godly lives in the light of this assured event. Jesus likewise told us to be ready for His coming, like faithful, diligent servants awaiting their master's return, or wise virgins having their lamps lit for the coming bridegroom. Let every day be lived in the light of His appearing so that we do not grow slack or indifferent to the reality of our salvation. We are to serve the Lord, to watch and to pray.

This is not a call either to fear or to religious legalism. Rather, it is a call to prepare for the greatest celebration ever. You have the invitation – RSVP!

Seeing Jesus in the Scriptures

Many people fear the day of judgment and doubt whether they will escape hell. We have one certain hope: Jesus bore the wrath of God in our place. The price is paid, and there is no further need of an offering or a punishment for sin for all those who put their faith in the sufficiency of His death. This truth should fill us not with anxiety but with the profoundest gratitude.

The return of Christ is an event to be anticipated with joy, for it will mark the end of all evil and the inauguration of a new world of peace and blessing for all His people. Jesus will see the fruit of the suffering of His soul and be satisfied.

WEEK 3

The Call of God

Opening Icebreaker

Share brief testimonies of the call of God on your lives. To avoid long-windedness use a timer with a maximum of two or three minutes per person. If some are not sure, then maybe you could suggest ways that you have seen God move in their lives.

Bible Readings

Isaiah 6:1–13   Romans 6:17–19
Revelation 4:1–11   1 John 1:8–10
Matthew 13:11–17

Key verse: 'Then I heard the voice of the Lord saying, "Whom shall I send? And who will go for us?" And I said, "Here am I. Send me!"' Isaiah 6:8

Focus: Salvation by grace invites service inspired by gratitude.

Opening Our Eyes

Any true call of God begins with a revelation of God. Such revelations most likely come to those people who in their innermost being are already seeking Him.

Isaiah's vision took place during the year of King Uzziah's death, c.740 BC. Like Daniel, Ezekiel and the apostle John, who each had similar experiences, the vision is royal and priestly – the Lord is king and His robe fills the temple. Fiery, six-winged creatures called seraphim herald God's praises. Seraphim are connected with fire and with the holy justice of God. They declare with earthshaking force that God is exalted, all-holy, all-powerful and His glory fills the earth.

Such an intense awareness of God's holiness convicts Isaiah of his mortality and of his sinfulness. He is doomed. There is no hope for him or for his people. The apostle Peter had a similar experience in the presence of Jesus; '... he fell at Jesus' knees and said, "Go away from me, Lord; I am a sinful man!"' (Luke 5:8).

Isaiah is especially convicted over his speech. Jesus reminds us that our words originate from our inner being: 'You brood of vipers, how can you who are evil say anything good? For out of the overflow of the heart the mouth speaks' (Matt. 12:34).

The prophet expects judgment but instead he finds grace. One of the seraphim takes a live coal and touches it to his lips. There are no works required. The confession of sin is sufficient. God initiates Isaiah's cleansing, for there was nothing he could do to make himself acceptable to the Lord. At this point, Isaiah is justified by faith. All his guilt is removed. Atonement has been made.

Salvation should always lead to service and the newly
redeemed Isaiah hears God's voice. The invitation to serve
comes from God, the Father, Son and Holy Spirit: 'Whom
shall I send? And who will go for us?'

The prophet's response is immediate. 'Here am I. Send
me!' It is a response reiterated by God's servants down
the centuries. Service does not save, and it is never
compelled. It is the grateful dedication of those who
know they have received grace and mercy. 'For we are
God's workmanship, created in Christ Jesus to do good
works, which God prepared in advance for us to do'
(Eph. 2:10).

Isaiah's cleansed lips will from now on be used to
proclaim the word of the Lord. It will be a thankless task.
Although Isaiah's words are today sung and spoken all
over the earth, in his lifetime he was to have no success.
Indeed, his preaching would serve to harden the hearts of
the people, for every time we refuse or resist God's word
it becomes that little bit more difficult to respond the next
time we hear it. There is heavy irony in the Lord's word:
'Go on, make them callous, otherwise they might just turn
to me and be healed!' (see Isa. 6:9–10). Jesus took the
same provocative line in His day (see Matt. 13:13–15).

Isaiah wants to know how long he must do this. Until
the whole nation is overrun and destroyed and ninety
per cent of the people are either killed or taken into
captivity – and even the remaining ten per cent will be all
but destroyed in a further bout of judgment. Is there any
hope? Yes. It is invested in a tiny remnant, a few chosen
ones, in whose hearts and loins resides the holy seed.
Even though the tree is fallen the stump will grow again.

Discussion Starters

1. How do you think we might prepare our hearts to receive the revelation of God?

2. What do you understand by the term 'the holiness of God'?

3. Discuss why true conviction of sin can only come from a revelation of God's holiness.

4. Isaiah experienced salvation by grace. How do you explain this to your not-yet-believing friends and neighbours?

5. What really motivates you to serve the Lord? Is it guilt, duty or gratitude?

_____

_____

_____

_____

_____

6. We all like instant results, but proclaiming God's word is like sowing seed. What encouragement can you take to persevere in the seed sowing process?

_____

_____

_____

_____

_____

7. God's investment for the future was in the holy remnant. What bearing does this have on our understanding of the Church and its witness today?

_____

_____

_____

_____

_____

Personal Application

Have you reached the place where you know that before God there is nothing good about you and all your righteousness is like filthy rags in His sight? Acknowledging your sin at the foot of the cross, have you received the holy touch that takes away all your sin and uncleanness? Do you know that you are justified by faith? These are vital questions for each of us, for without being able to answer 'yes' to them we are still lost and under judgment.

Have you also responded to God's call to devote your life to serving Him in whatever calling He gives you? There are many different ways of proclaiming God's word. Full-time preaching is only one of them. All of us who are redeemed are full-time missionaries every time we leave our homes, and sometimes even before that. Is this how you view yourself?

Seeing Jesus in the Scriptures

The holy justice of God demands that the sinner pays for his sin. Jesus, the sinless Son of God, graciously and willingly became sin for us. 'God presented him as a sacrifice of atonement, through faith in his blood' (Rom. 3:25). The price is paid. No other sacrifice is required. Penitent sinners are justified by simple faith in Christ's atoning work. The altar is Calvary and the fire is the holy touch of God that applies the precious blood of Christ to our unclean lives and declares us cleansed.

Give thanks to the Lord for His wonderful salvation. We should never get over it, but serve Him with gratitude throughout our days.

WEEK 4

Call His Name Immanuel

Opening Icebreaker

Never mind the season – sing or read some of the great Christmas carols that talk about who Jesus is. Which ones are your favourites and why?

Bible Readings

Isaiah 7:1–14	Matthew 4:12–17
Matthew 1:18–25	Isaiah 11:1–5
Isaiah 9:1–7	Zechariah 3:8–9

Key verse: '… The virgin will be with child and will give birth to a son, and will call him Immanuel.' Isaiah 7:14

Focus: God's sure purposes are vested in the Messiah.

Opening Our Eyes

Three prophecies lie at the heart of Isaiah's vision of hope. They are set within the context of sin and judgment. The first is triggered by a fresh outbreak of civil war between the northern and the southern kingdoms. In 732 BC, a military alliance between Aram and Israel marched against Jerusalem. Isaiah and his son, Shearjashub (A Remnant Will Return), advised King Ahaz not to panic but to seek a sign from God. Ahaz petulantly refused the invitation, so God declared that He would send His own sign: a virgin will become pregnant, give birth to a son and call His name Immanuel – God with us.

The prophecy was a dire warning. Assyria will invade the region, destroying Israel and Aram, and in the process reducing Judah to a subsistence level. This will occur within the time it takes for a virgin to conceive and raise a child to the years of understanding.

The second of these prophecies points to a future restoration of honour to the devastated north, to Galilee in particular. Light shines in the darkness, harvest celebrations ring out; as in Gideon's time, the oppressor is defeated and the yoke of enslavement broken. A child is born: a king, but no ordinary king. This Man has divine attributes – He is the Wonderful Counsellor, the Mighty God, the Everlasting Father, the Prince of Peace. He is David's true Descendant and His reign will last for ever.

The third prophecy connects us with the remnant stump of David's line. From an almost destroyed ancestry will sprout a fruitful Branch. This Man will be characterised by wisdom, power and knowledge, and the fear of the Lord. He will institute social justice and will destroy the wicked. Ecological harmony will flow from His reign and the whole earth will be filled with the knowledge of the Lord as the waters cover the sea. He will be a rallying point for all nations and He will recall the remnant of His people from all across the earth. The power of Egypt and of Assyria will be shattered. Zechariah adds to this prophecy many years later. The Branch will remove the sins of God's people in a single day – a powerful anticipation of the atonement wrought by Christ at Calvary.

These three prophecies combine to form the Messianic hope of God's people. Whatever their immediate meaning, they point unequivocally to Jesus of Nazareth – to both His first and His second advents. It is a fine example of prophecy having more than one partial fulfilment, and in this case the final picture will not be complete until Christ returns and inaugurates a new heaven and a new earth.

The Child, the King, the Branch. God incarnate, God reigning, God redeeming. Christ our hope, our Lord, and our Saviour. However oppressed God's people may feel, however uncertain the times, God is with us. His prophetic purpose came to pass in Isaiah's day and in the first coming of Christ to the world. The remaining fulfilment of the prophecies will not fail. The nations are gathering to Christ and the earth is being filled with the glory of God. Christ will come again, and every knee will bow, acknowledging that He is King of kings and Lord of lords. Says the Lord of His word, 'It will not return to me empty, but will accomplish what I desire and achieve the purpose for which I sent it' (Isa. 55:11).

Discussion Starters

1. What relevance do the titles of Jesus, 'Wonderful Counsellor, Mighty God, Everlasting Father, Prince of Peace', have to your life and to the lives of your neighbours?

2. What do you expect to happen when you pray, 'Your kingdom come'?

3. How would you use these prophecies and the Gospel of Matthew to demonstrate to a Jewish friend that Jesus is the long-awaited Messiah?

4. Why is the virgin conception of Christ such an important truth?

5. How do these far-reaching prophecies encourage us as we look at the world scene today?

_____

_____

_____

_____

6. What personal encouragement can you take from the fact that your life is in the prophetic purposes of God?

_____

_____

_____

_____

7. What do you understand by the word 'atonement'? How important is this to our salvation and to how we live?

_____

_____

_____

_____

Personal Application

God knows what He is doing! A thousand years is nothing in the sight of the One who knows the beginning from the end and whose purposes are from eternity to eternity. Surely then He knows all about our lives and circumstances. The psalmist says, 'For you created my inmost being; you knit me together in my mother's womb ... your eyes saw my unformed body. All the days ordained for me were written in your book before one of them came to be' (Psa. 139:13,16). The Lord of history is also the Lord of our story.

Miraculously and undeterred, God brought salvation to the world through the unruly story of His people. It is the same with us; '... we know that in all things God works for the good of those who love him, who have been called according to his purpose' (Rom. 8:28).

Seeing Jesus in the Scriptures

Isaiah's prophecy of a coming Messiah found its fulfilment on the day when the Spirit of God descended upon a young virgin named Mary. Her child is the holy Son of God, untainted by Adam's sin and yet able to save us from our own transgressions. Jesus would inherit David's throne, but His kingdom would be unlike that of the world's rulers. He would be the Servant King, laying down His life for us and winning our hearts with His sacrificial love.

This same Jesus is now at the right hand of the Father. Already, He has begun to reign. Praise God for His first coming, and pray for His return when the kingdom fully comes.

WEEK 5

Judge of the Whole Earth

Opening Icebreaker

Each member of the group takes the opportunity to say, 'If I ruled the world, I would ...' Choose one frivolous thing that you would change or implement, and one serious one.

Bible Readings

Isaiah 10:1–13   Revelation 5:1–14
Isaiah 14:12–15   Psalm 2:1–12
Isaiah 24:18–23

Key verses: 'Woe to the Assyrian, the rod of my anger, in whose hand is the club of my wrath! ...' Isaiah 10:5–7

Focus: The politics of man are subject to the purposes of God.

Opening Our Eyes

A significant section of Isaiah is concerned with the international politics of God. Although the focus is on the Middle East, Isaiah's God is no local or national deity; He is the Lord of history and the Judge of the whole earth. Whatever the politics of man, a greater power and purpose is at work, and we cannot make sense of history without understanding it.

Assyria is a case in point. The nation was expanding its empire and had subdued everything westwards, including Israel and most of Judah. Humanly, it's the usual story of ambition, power, wealth and self-interest, yet Assyria is only permitted its advance so that God can use it to purify His wayward people from their destructive idolatry. The viciousness with which Assyria did this, and their imperial ambitions, went beyond God's intent. 'Woe to the Assyrian, the rod of my anger, in whose hand is the club of my wrath! I send him against a godless nation, I dispatch him against a people who anger me ... But this is not what he intends, this is not what he has in mind; his purpose is to destroy, to put an end to many nations' (Isa. 10:5–7). For this imperial arrogance, God will punish Assyria and reduce it from a great forest to a small copse.

Assyria was an immediate threat, but another lay on the horizon of history. Babylon, the weak Chaldean kingdom, would rise to great power. It, too, will be an instrument of divine judgment against God's people. Jerusalem will be destroyed and its people taken into captivity until they learn to renounce their idols and keep the covenant. Babylon will also prove arrogant and the empire will fall, this time to the Medes. Against all the odds, God's people will be restored to their land.

This is not just ancient history. Babylon becomes a byword for the empire spirit and Isaiah's prophecies leap

across the centuries to the Roman Empire and then to the
great Babylon of the book of Revelation, and the end of
the world. Isaiah foresees the break-up of the planet, the
destruction of the armies of the world and the dissolution
of the stars of heaven. He is prophesying our today and
tomorrow!

Why do these proud empires rise to rule the world?
What lies behind them? The answer is given with reference
to Babylon, but it applies to all empires. Lucifer, the
rebel prince of this world, whose arrogance laid claim
to equality with God Himself, is the inspiration for the
rapacity, idolatry and ambition of the empire builders.
A satanic spirit inspires them, but it will not last for ever.
Satan was cast out of heaven, and his time on earth is
short. The day will dawn when the Son of God will
destroy his works and cast him into the lake of eternal fire.

Israel was surrounded by enemies who either allied
themselves with the invading empire or themselves harried
God's people. Moab, Philistia, Edom, Damascus, Cush,
Egypt, Tyre, Arabia are among those whose malice the
Lord notes. Furthermore, Israel, Judah, and Jerusalem itself,
have become enemies of the truth and servants of demonic
idols. None of them will be spared the fury of the Lord
when He rises to vindicate His faithful remnant. Out of
these apocalyptic events the Lord will fulfil His promise to
bring forth His ransomed people. Through them will come
the Saviour of the world and the Light to the nations.

Discussion Starters

1. Where do you get your political beliefs from? Is it from the perspective of Jesus as the Lord of the nations, or from elsewhere?

2. What do you think are the characteristics of the satanic empire spirit?

3. The empire spirit is always contrary to the will of God. Discuss the practical implications of this in the light of the kingdom of God.

4. How do we interpret the events in current world politics without simply arguing over speculative opinions? What is our real task? See 1 Timothy 2:1–4.

5. What do you understand by the term, 'the kingdom of God'? How does this find its practical outworking in your local church?

_____

_____

_____

_____

6. How may we best focus our eyes on Jesus in the face of world events?

_____

_____

_____

_____

7. In what ways has Jesus conquered Satan's power? How does that help you live your life?

_____

_____

_____

_____

Personal Application

At the sound of the seventh trumpet loud voices declare, 'The kingdom of the world has become the kingdom of our Lord and of his Christ, and he will reign for ever and ever' (Rev. 11:15). We may be in this world but we belong to a different kingdom – one that will ultimately subdue all the satanic arrogance, injustice and corruption of the world's rulers. Every time we pray, 'Your kingdom come,' we hasten the advance of Christ's rule over the nations.

We are already citizens of that kingdom and by our life and witness, both individually and corporately, we demonstrate the glory of what it is like to live under the government of our Lord Jesus.

Seeing Jesus in the Scriptures

History is His story. The purification and preservation of the line of promise brought forth the Messiah. Jesus is the pivotal point of world history. Everything led to Him; everything proceeds from Him. He is the Alpha and Omega, the beginning and the end. He is the Heir to the nations, the One who holds the scroll and who unlooses the seals; '... he must reign until he has put all his enemies under his feet' (1 Cor. 15:25).

'In putting everything under him, God left nothing that is not subject to him. Yet at present we do not see everything subject to him. But we see Jesus, who was made a little lower than the angels, now crowned with glory and honour ...' (Heb. 2:8–9). True worshippers focus their eyes on Jesus and know that the future is safe in His hands.

WEEK 6

Songs of Deliverance

Opening Icebreaker

What is it about your salvation that makes you deliriously happy? Invite each other to share one aspect of God's grace and why it particularly makes you so excited.

Bible Readings

Isaiah 12:1–6	Ephesians 2:14–22
Isaiah 35:1–10	Ephesians 5:19–20
1 Peter 1:8–9; 2:9	Matthew 28:16–20

Key verse: 'Shout aloud and sing for joy, people of Zion, for great is the Holy One of Israel among you.' Isaiah 12:6

Focus: Salvation fills our hearts and our mouths with unabashed praise and thanksgiving.

Opening Our Eyes

The greater part of Isaiah's prophecies are written in a poetic form capable of being read, sung or chanted. The two songs before us celebrate the Lord's mighty deliverance following a time of trial and exile.

Chapter 12 records Isaiah's personal response to the Messiah's appearing. The Root of David becomes the rallying point for the nations. Astonishingly, He who gathers His people from exile – a miracle in itself – will perform a second and even more remarkable gathering. He will call out His elect from all the nations of the world and He will bring them into a glorious unity as one new holy nation. As Peter explains, the prophets were predicting the sacrifice of Christ and the birth of the Church (1 Pet. 1:10–12). This, according to Paul, is the great mystery that was revealed to the apostles and prophets (Eph. 2:11–21; 3:6). Anticipating this glorious day, Isaiah cannot contain himself. He bursts into praise. God is his salvation, his strength and his song. Faith replaces fear. The wells of salvation are open; come drink with joy!

Isaiah is the great missionary prophet. Anticipating the command of Jesus to go into all the world and preach the gospel, he urges a thankful people to proclaim the Lord's glory throughout all nations. We are gathered so that we may be sent (1 Pet. 2:9). The Church is to celebrate – noisily so – but it is to do so as a missionary church. God is in the midst of us when we are in the midst of the world! Astounding as it seemed in Isaiah's day, in our own time the word is coming to pass: 'From the ends of the earth we hear singing: "Glory to the Righteous One"' (Isa. 24:16).

Travelling across the wilderness is never easy. Difficult terrain, the absence of water, a burning sun, predatory wild animals and the ever present threat of bandits make it a daunting journey for those returning to Zion. Yet the desert will be transformed, declares Isaiah (Isa. 35:1–10). Water will flow and the barren land will become a fertile plain. The frail, the elderly and the fearful will have reason to rejoice, for God is on the move. They will see His glory as He destroys their enemies and saves them. A day of miraculous healing will dawn; barrenness will turn to fruitfulness as water floods the desert. As Jesus said of the coming Holy Spirit, 'If anyone is thirsty, let him come to me and drink. Whoever believes in me, as the Scripture has said, streams of living water will flow from within him' (John 7:37–38).

The wilderness is a rough place but its divine transformation will include the provision of a highway – a holy way for a holy people. No one need fear taking this salvation road: the unclean with their corrupting ways cannot walk it; nor can the wicked fools who deny God and lead people astray; and nor can the devil. That roaring predatory lion will be kept at bay. This is the road for the redeemed. The ransom price has been paid by God Himself, for the Messiah is also the suffering servant – 'For even the Son of Man did not come to be served, but to serve, and to give his life as a ransom for many' (Mark 10:45). Such people will enter Zion with singing and with an onrush of joy that will banish all misery.

Discussion Starters

1. Discuss the extent of the power of the cross to break down all the barriers of race, class and gender erected by man. How well does this work out in your church?

2. Are your praises confined to Sundays and to in-house environments? How do you proclaim the Lord's praises in your daily life and witness?

3. Why is our praise and thanksgiving so often lacking the vibrancy and fervour of the redeemed? What do you think it takes to stir us up?

4. Believers have sometimes divided the work of the Holy Spirit between power for service and holiness for living. Why is this a mistake? What has Isaiah 35 to teach us about this?

5. How would you explain to an unbeliever what it means for the desert to become a place of fruitfulness? Give practical examples of how this has proved true in your own life.

_____

_____

_____

_____

6. How is it possible to walk this holy road to heaven and yet still live a normal life in the world?

_____

_____

_____

_____

7. How do you assess the holiness of your life? Is it on a plus/minus scale of behaviour, or is it assessed by the reality of your walk with the Lord and your desire to please Him?

_____

_____

_____

_____

Personal Application

Our human need for water provides a powerful metaphor for the slaking of our spiritual thirst. After a period of spiritual captivity and desert wanderings, what joy there is to discover the refreshing depths of renewal in the Lord. Even though we may have gone into self-induced bondage, like the prodigal son, as soon as we repent we will be welcomed back to Zion and to a celebratory feast.

It is easy to doubt this. Will the Lord have me back? Can I ever make it? Surely I am too damaged? Isaiah says to our doubts, 'Be strong, do not fear.' Whatever the situation, God can turn our mourning into dancing. He can bring us such joy that the former gloom will be like a night that vanishes in the light of the rising sun.

Seeing Jesus in the Scriptures

The way of holiness isn't a technique for living, or a particular set of devotional exercises, and even less is it a list of dos and don'ts. The Way is a Person, and His name is Jesus. He is the Holy One, and as we live in Him and contemplate Him, so we are progressively changed into His likeness. Journeying through life in companionship with Him is the true key to overcoming the world, the flesh and the devil. People who do so have set their sights on the heavenly Zion where one day all evil will be banished and we shall see Jesus as He really is. We will have arrived home, safe, sound and perfected in holiness to be just like Him.

WEEK 7

Overcoming the Enemy

Opening Icebreaker

Recount times when you were really afraid and someone got you out of trouble. How did you feel afterwards?

Bible Readings

Isaiah 36:1–37:38
(if short of time,
just read together
37:14–38)
Psalm 18:1–6

Psalm 110:1–7
Isaiah 26:1–5
Ephesians 6:10–18
Revelation 19:11–16

Key verse: 'I will defend this city and save it, for my sake and for the sake of David my servant!' Isaiah 37:35

Focus: The Lord is our Rock, our Fortress and our Deliverer.

Opening Our Eyes

The long-dreaded day had arrived. Jerusalem was under siege to the vast, invincible Assyrian army. Fighting was out of the question. The enemy was too strong. Hired support from Egypt was as useless as using a twig for a walking stick! A major water supply had been blockaded. The choice was simple: surrender and be deported, or hold out until the terrible end – which would mean famine, slaughter, rape, pillage, fire and ruin, the destruction of the temple, the end of monotheistic faith.

There was one other option: prayer and prophecy. Hezekiah sought the Lord. His prayer affirmed two realities. First, that the living God of Israel was also God over all the nations. Indeed, He was the Creator of the entire universe. Second, there was a real and present danger that could not be disregarded. Blasphemous Sennacherib had destroyed other nations and their gods (albeit they were no more than man-made idols), and dared to claim that God had sent him to conquer Jerusalem. Now he was at the gates of the city. Hezekiah entreated the Holy One of Israel to deliver His people so that all nations would know that He alone was God.

The Lord's response came through Isaiah. It was a message of uncompromising confidence. Zion, like a defiant young girl, tosses her head in scorn as mighty Sennacherib flees for his life. His blasphemous boasts are worthless. He only got this far because the Lord ordained it. How dare he insult the Holy One of Israel by claiming credit? No way is he going to enter this city. 'I will defend it,' says the Lord. There will be no famine and no starvation; for two years the land will yield enough of itself and in the third year farming can recommence. The people, like the land, will root and fruit. This besieged remnant will emerge from the city and multiply in the land once again. God's purpose will not be thwarted.

It seemed an impossible hope but one should never underestimate the power of angels. In one night, the Angel of the Lord slaughtered 185,000 Assyrian troops, and the morning saw bodies lying everywhere. Sennacherib returned at once to Nineveh and in due time was assassinated by his own sons while worshipping his useless god, Nisroch. Jerusalem was saved and the faithful remnant people who carried the Messianic line in their genes and in their hearts were spared. The Lord proved true to His promise, demonstrating once again that He answers prayer and defends His people. Truly, He is our Rock, our Fortress and our Deliverer.

There is a postscript to all this. Following the victory, Hezekiah became mortally ill and was told by Isaiah that he would die. Once again, he prayed. God heard his prayer and miraculously reversed the sundial as a sign of merciful healing, giving the king fifteen more years. News of his recovery reached Babylon and when envoys came bearing gifts, Hezekiah foolishly showed them all his wealth. Isaiah was distraught at the news and prophesied that one day the Babylonians would return to defeat Jerusalem and to carry the people and the treasure to Babylon. That it would not occur in Hezekiah's lifetime was small comfort to anyone.

However, hope there would be when the time came. Prophesying into the future, the next chapter of Isaiah opens with the words, 'Comfort, comfort my people, says your God' (Isa. 40:1). But that's another story!

Discussion Starters

1. In what ways do you find that the Lord is your Rock, your Fortress and your Deliverer?

2. What contrast can you draw between worship of the living God and the worship of idols in our own culture today?

3. What can we learn from Hezekiah's prayer about how we should pray?

4. Angels are ministering spirits sent forth on behalf of the elect. What do you consider this means for us today?

5. The Lord promises to supply the needs of His people so that they will not starve. Is this always true? How does it affect your own economic life? What about believers suffering persecution or famine?

_____

_____

_____

_____

6. In Matthew 7:6, Jesus tells us not to throw our pearls to pigs. Bearing in mind Hezekiah's mistake, what wisdom should we exercise in our own lives?

_____

_____

_____

_____

7. What comfort do you draw from the fact that Jesus will judge the nations in righteousness and will vindicate His oppressed people?

_____

_____

_____

_____

Personal Application

God has a prophetic word for every situation. Most commonly it will come from the Bible, and sometimes, if according to Scripture, through the mouths of others, or perhaps directly to our spirits. The precondition is that we seek God's face in prayer for the right reason. How will God be glorified and His name be vindicated? James says, for our encouragement, 'The prayer of a *righteous man* is powerful and effective' (James 5:16, my emphasis).

People who pray like this have no need to fear. As the psalmist declares, 'The LORD is my rock, my fortress and my deliverer ... I call to the LORD, who is worthy of praise, and I am saved from my enemies' (Psa. 18:2–3).

Seeing Jesus in the Scriptures

The Angel of the Lord is generally understood to be a pre-incarnate manifestation of Jesus. This is no 'gentle Jesus, meek and mild'. He is the warrior Christ, defending His people and putting down His enemies. The risen Christ will destroy 'all dominion, authority and power. For he must reign until he has put all his enemies under his feet. The last enemy to be destroyed is death' (1 Cor. 15:24–26). John's vision of Jesus reveals the Faithful and True on a white horse. From His mouth comes a sharp sword to strike down the nations, whom He rules with an iron sceptre.

Praise God, we have One who comes to vindicate and to deliver His oppressed people. Evil will not triumph while the Lord God Almighty reigns – and He shall reign for ever and ever!

Leader's Notes

Week 1: The National Disease

Isaiah's prophecy is a large book, so in these seven sessions we will deal with just the main themes of chapters 1–39. However, it will benefit you and your group members to read a chapter a day for the duration of the course. Although it is sometimes suggested that Isaiah was written by two or three different people at different times, there is no real evidence for this. Those who hold that view generally have already rejected the possibility of predictive prophecy – hardly a problem if we recognise that Isaiah was inspired by the God who knows the beginning from the end!

Read the Introduction to your group and, if possible, show them a map of the Assyrian Empire. Explain that the Assyrians were already conquering territory in Israel and Judah, and worse was threatened. This, Isaiah sees, is the judgment of God on a people who had broken the covenant by their idolatry and sinful behaviour.

The Opening Icebreaker is designed to make a connection between obvious sin and disease, for example, sexual promiscuity and chlamydia, drunken driving and road accidents. There are less obvious ones, like the proven connection between consumerism and depression. However, be careful not to condemn people who are sick for no reason of their own doing. Keep it general to society to emphasise the moral and spiritual sickness of the nation.

Each week, ask different people to do the readings, then read out the Opening Our Eyes section. This week's is mostly a summary of Isaiah 1 and it paints a vivid picture of decadence and corruption glossed over with religious hypocrisy. It is hard not to draw parallels with our contemporary society. Note the global injustice in which our nation participates to sustain our consumerism, our hedonistic celebrity culture, our obsession with fashion, youth and the body, our mockery of spiritual life, our dabbling with New Age occultism. Discussion Starter 1 will open this up and invite a response, and Discussion Starter 7 asks us to consider appropriate political engagement.

Isaiah challenges the religious hypocrisy that divorces conduct from worship, or assumes sin can be offset by ritual. Read Psalm 24:3–4 and using Discussion Starter 2 explore the reality of living pure lives before God. Discussion Starter 4 invites us to change our behaviour. Try to be practical: what do we need to give up, what have we neglected that we need to remedy? You may wish to set this in a time of prayer. Reading the Personal Application at this point will be helpful.

Grace is always available for the penitent. Read the Seeing Jesus section. This applies directly to our own lives, but then using Discussion Starter 5, ask how we can share this good news with those around us. Since good news is meaningless without experiencing the bad news it counteracts, use Discussion Starter 3 to ask how we communicate to our society the notion of divine justice and the consequences of sin.

Isaiah's hope for the future was vested in the remnant, a faithful group of people who rejected the prevailing culture and its decadent values in favour of God's ways. These people carried the Messianic hope in their hearts and anticipated the coming of Jesus. They were the true Church of their day. Discussion Starter 6 reminds us that faithful remnants can easily become quirky, inward-looking groups that have little connection with society. How can we live as God's holy people and yet still interact with the world around us? In other words, how can we be in the world, but not of the world?

Week 2: The Day of the Lord

You may wish to set yourself up in the role of the judge in the Opening Icebreaker. It is an opportunity for the group to reflect on the criminal state of mankind from God's point of view, eg *'I charge the world with* exploiting the poor ... with waging endless wars ... with persecuting the Church ... etc.

Isaiah confronts the nation with the imminence of the Day of the Lord – Judgment Day. It marks the collapse of society and of the ecosystem. The world will end dramatically. Isaiah's prophecies often unfold in different stages and this is a typical example. There was a fulfilment of this prophecy, partly in the eighth century BC and even more so at the fall of Jerusalem in 587 BC, but there was a further fulfilment in AD 70 when Jerusalem fell to the Romans. However, the culmination of this prophecy is still to come and will occur when Jesus returns in glory.

The notion of the Judgment Day conjures up mythical images of hellfire preachers and quaking sinners, yet we humans share a universal longing for justice. This is God-given, and surely God has the right to judge the world. As for demonstrating His wrath when He does so, do we really think He should be smiling benignly when He judges the corrupters of power, the torturers, rapists, child abusers and murderers who often otherwise escape justice? This is to say nothing of the lesser evils that dwell in the average human heart. Where does a righteous, impartial Judge draw the line? Use Discussion Starters 1 and 2 to explore this and come up with effective ways of communicating the idea.

The Christian gospel focuses on the Person and work of Christ, particularly in regard to the cross. Some have accused God of cosmic child abuse for pouring out His wrath on His Son. That is a gross distortion of the doctrine of substitutionary atonement. Jesus willingly took our place and bore the wrath due to us so that we might be justified by faith and be delivered from judgment. Indeed, God was in Christ, reconciling the world to Himself. Use Discussion Starter 3 to talk about this.

Bear in mind that some people secretly fear that they are beyond hope. Talk of judgment may accentuate those fears. You should address this by stressing the completeness and sufficiency of Christ's work. Read the Seeing Jesus section as you tackle Discussion Starter 4.

Many people seriously consider that the world is reaching its sell-by date and will end quite soon. Discussion Starters 5 and 6 provide an opportunity to speak about Christian hope. Jesus is coming back; that is the most certain fact about the future. It is not something to fear, but an event to anticipate with joy, for it will initiate the mending and transformation of all that is wrong. The peace and harmony that we long for will become a reality.

All life and existence follows the up-down-up waveform. In biblical terms, this is the life–death–resurrection pattern experienced by Jesus, and the pattern for how spiritual life works in the lives of His followers. Similarly, the present life of the world must end in the death of judgment, but the coming of Christ assures us of a resurrected new universe. Our conduct should reflect this hope. Read the Personal Application at this point, stressing that this is not intended to frighten us but to inspire us.

End this session by using Discussion Starter 7 to dream a little about what it will be like in the new heaven and earth.

Week 3: The Call of God

The Opening Icebreaker provides an opportunity for people to talk about their conversion experience and their sense of calling. Some people won't think they have a call on their lives – a misunderstanding that this session will help correct. Others will be very clear, and possibly long-winded. Use a timer and insist that everyone respects it!

Isaiah's vision was very vivid and visual, but a revelation of God is not necessarily a divine video clip. Some people have very visual minds and may see and hear God in this way. Others receive more of a divine impression, a spiritual sense of the Lord's presence and glory without any visual experience. Both are equally valid. Using Discussion Starter 1, encourage your group to seek the Lord continually and to be open to revelations of His glory however they come.

A mark of any true revelation is a conviction of the fear of the Lord – a wondrous scary awe that both attracts us and frightens us. Like Isaiah, we will be confronted with the truth about our sinful behaviour and our mortality. It is this humble acknowledgement of our need, and that of those around us, that releases God's cleansing power into our lives. Discussion Starters 2 and 3 invite us to talk about holiness and sin. God's holiness is not only absolute purity but the total otherness of the uncreated Creator. The seraphim (fiery ones) emphasise this by their words and their association with the purifying fire. Don't spend too much time speculating about these heavenly beings. They are close to God's throne, and they declare

His worth, just like the living creatures in Revelation 4.

Although it is likely that most of your group are believers, some may not have a clear experience of salvation and, in any case, each of us needs to know how to communicate the gospel of grace with our life-neighbours. Read the Personal Application and, along with Discussion Starter 4, try to clarify your understanding of the vital truths of atonement and justification by faith. Read the Seeing Jesus section and invite your group members to consider their own standing before God. All of us should be thankful; some may yield their lives to the Lord and enter the joy of salvation during this session.

We are not saved *by* service but we are called *to* service. Everyone who experiences Christ's salvation is called to be a full-time missionary, whatever their sphere of life may be. 'Here am I; send me' is that natural response of the true believer. Use Discussion Starter 5 to check out your motives for serving God. Guilt and glamour are bad motives. Encourage people to serve the Lord from a grateful heart.

Isaiah's call was not an easy one and nor is ours. Given the spiritual famine in our land, we will spend a good deal of time ploughing and sowing seed. There will be disappointments and hardship, but that doesn't mean we have necessarily got it wrong. Explain this using Discussion Starter 6. In every generation the Lord has His faithful remnant who carry the holy seed within their hearts. Using Discussion Starter 7, consider how that outworks in your own church. Stress the importance of our identity as God's chosen people who are entrusted with the truth of the gospel. Remind your group members that faithfulness means full-of-faith-ness and is much more than mere stoical perseverance. Remind yourselves also that God is faithful and that if we do not give up, in due season, He will honour our labours.

Week 4: Call His Name Immanuel

Who needs an excuse for Christmas? Whatever time of
year you are doing this study you can still sing some
great Christmas carols. Get each member of the group to
choose a favourite and to explain why. You won't have
time to sing them all, but you could have a show of
hands and sing the most popular.

This session concentrates on three of Isaiah's prophecies
and their fulfilment. These prophecies are at the heart of
his vision of hope, for Isaiah anticipated the coming of
the Messiah. *Messiah* is the Hebrew for Christ and means
'the Anointed One'.

As we have noted, many of Isaiah's prophecies have more
than one partial fulfilment before the whole revelation
comes to pass. Some of them have yet to reach that point.
You should again explain this principle to your group.

The first prophecy is occasioned by another outbreak
of civil war. Explain how the nation split between north
and south – Israel and Judah – following Solomon's
death. Ahaz refuses to seek for a sign because he is
resentful against God. God gives a sign anyway. Within
a few years, from virginity, through conception, birth
and childhood, the enemy power will be broken, but it
will be broken by a worse foe – Assyria. Yet, the child is
called Immanuel and is the Messiah – or is he? Matthew
quotes this passage to demonstrate 730 years later that
Jesus is the Messiah. Discussion Starter 4 will allow you
to talk about the virgin conception of Christ. If Jesus is
not conceived by the Holy Spirit then He is just a better
version of one of us, under the curse of Adam's sin.
Because He is conceived of God, He is free from that
taint and able to offer Himself as an unblemished lamb

for our sins. Read the Seeing Jesus section at this point.

The second prophecy is one of liberation, but the Messiah does not originate from the privileged south. He comes from the despised north, from a land already ravaged by Assyria. Use Discussion Starter 1 to expand your understanding of His titles. Again, Matthew quotes this passage in connection with Jesus, this time at the commencement of His Galilean ministry. Use Discussion Starter 3 to explore how to reach Jews with this good news.

The third prophecy reminds us of Isaiah's calling, and the remnant stump that will sprout again. The faithful Branch will institute justice for the poor and will usher in a reign of peace and harmony. Using Discussion Starter 2, ask people what they expect when they pray, 'Your kingdom come.'

The Branch will remove sins in one day. This was dramatically fulfilled when Jesus died for us. Discussion Starter 7 gives us a second opportunity to talk about atonement. The word literally means, 'at-one-ment'.

God is gathering His people from every nation through the message of the gospel and in anticipation of the second coming of Christ. This news hardly ever makes the headlines but it is what really matters. Discussion Starter 5 invites us to interpret world events in the light of this. God is working His purposes out and we should be encouraged!

Prophecies that span the centuries remind us that God knows the end from the beginning. He also knows all about us. Read the Personal Application and with the aid of Discussion Starter 6 talk about the way in which our lives are in God's prophetic purposes, even though mostly they are lived at the apparently mundane level. The Lord of history is also the Lord of our story.

Week 5: Judge of the Whole Earth

The Opening Icebreaker is fun with a serious intent.
What would you do if you ruled the world? Each member
chooses a silly thing like, 'I'd make chocolate free,' and a
serious thing, like 'I'd abolish Third World debt'.

This session is about the international politics of God.
Politics and religion must go together – it all depends
on what politics and what religion. The bulk of Isaiah's
prophecy is taken up with God's actions in human affairs.
Since this must be the most important political reality
you may well wonder why our politicians and statesmen
ignore it! Discussion Starter 1 invites us to examine our
own political beliefs. Do they come from God or are
they just our social class or family preference, or are they
merely humanistic? It's no use calling Jesus Lord and then
acting as though that great fact was not relevant to the
international political arena.

Assyria's military expansion had made it the dominant
world power during Isaiah's ministry. God allowed this
to happen to chastise His rebel people, but Assyria saw
it differently. They had conquered; they were the empire;
there was no limit to their arrogance and ambition. Use
Discussion Starters 2 and 3 to identify the characteristics
of the empire spirit and its inevitable conflict with the
kingdom of God. Why did Jesus say, 'My kingdom is not
of this world' (John 18:36)? What are the different values
of Christ's kingdom? Remind people that it is not just our
enemies who may be guilty of empire building.

No doubt members of your group will have their own
take on world politics and you must be careful not to let
your meeting degenerate into a political argument. We are
reminded in 1 Timothy 2:1–4 of our specific political role

and it would be good if you put this into practice during the meeting.

Isaiah foresaw the fall of Assyria and the rise of Babylon. He also saw that Satan, Lucifer, was the hidden inspiration behind the empire and its allies. The apostle John develops the theme in the book of Revelation, contrasting Babylon and the Great Prostitute with the kingdom of God and the Bride of Christ. Although the Church is not the full extent of the kingdom of God it is called to express and advance it. Using Discussion Starter 5 invite suggestions as to how this works in practice. You might like to draw a parallel between a national culture and the culture of Christ's people. As an alien visitor, what would you expect to find regarding language, customs, attitudes?

Once again, it is the faithful remnant who, in spite of all setbacks and opposition, hold on to the word of God. The Lord came, as God had promised – and the Lord will come again, as the Lord has promised! He will keep faith with His people. Read the Personal Application and using Discussion Starter 6 explore how we look to Jesus. You might suggest that we should be reading about His lordship, focusing on Him in prayer, declaring His victory, and praying for His return.

Evidently, we do not see every knee bowing to Jesus just yet. But we do see Him reigning and in control of world events – see Revelation 5:9–10. Read the Seeing Jesus section and with the help of Discussion Starter 7 end your session reflecting on the victory of Christ over Satan – at Calvary, in our world today, and when He returns in glory. Ask what difference that makes to our personal circumstances and perhaps take time to pray into those circumstances together.

Week 6: Songs of Deliverance

Scripture teaches us that those who have experienced
the Lord's salvation are supremely happy and, in spite of
circumstances, are often overwhelmed with thanksgiving
and praise. The Opening Icebreaker provides an
opportunity for each member of your group to speak
about one aspect of their salvation that fills them with joy.
Be aware that people express their emotions in different
ways and not all do so with the same outward enthusiasm.
That isn't too important; it's the heart that counts.

The NIV and many other versions indicate where the text
is written in poetic form by indenting it. You will see
from this that most of Isaiah's prophecies were delivered
as poetry. In this session we concentrate on two poetic
songs that celebrate God's deliverance of His people.

In chapter 12, Isaiah prophesies into the distant future
to a time when God will bring His people back from
Babylonian exile. In the same breath, he also prophesies a
second gathering, a gathering of the elect from all nations.
The New Testament writers clearly understood this to refer
to the global spread of the gospel and the consequent
emergence of the one holy nation, the Church of Christ
in which all human divisions are abolished. Thrilled with
anticipation, Isaiah bursts into a paean of praise. Use
Discussion Starter 1 to examine how well the uniting power
of the cross is outworking in your own church situation. Is
there more you should be doing to facilitate this?

Praise and thanksgiving are a vital aspect of our witness.
Using Discussion Starters 2 and 3 explore how we can
keep the flame burning, not just in church, but every day
in our workplaces. Don't be distracted into criticising the
music! Praise is much more than half an hour's corporate

singing. Focus on the way the Holy Spirit stirs up the wellsprings of the heart and the missionary impact that a praising people have in society.

The second song in Isaiah 35 is about the transformation of the wilderness into a place of fertility and easy travel. The once barren and daunting terrain will become a land of miraculous healing and refreshment as well as a path of holiness. Use Discussion Starter 4 to remind one another that power and holiness go together and we should not partition the work of the Holy Spirit. Give examples of healing miracles in your church and of sinful lives becoming holy lives.

We inhabit a land of parched souls and polluted wells. Discussion Starter 5 invites us to explore how we might communicate to unbelievers the wondrous transformation that has occurred in our hearts as a result of the gospel. Some members of your group may be feeling personally barren at present. Read the Personal Application and encourage them to receive again the joy of the Lord.

The holy road is not a tightrope where at any moment we might lose our balance and tumble into sin! It is a safe path for pilgrims, rather than a carefully controlled code of practise with penalties attached. Read the Seeing Jesus section so that people understand that Jesus is the Road and real holiness is about travelling through life in fellowship with Him. Discuss what this means in practice with the aid of Discussion Starters 6 and 7. Finish by reminding folk that this road has a heavenly destination. We shall one day enter Zion singing with joy. You may wish to end this session with a time of praise and thanksgiving and by giving folk the opportunity to refresh their souls in the presence of the Lord.

Week 7: Overcoming the Enemy

Mortal fear – fear of death, pain, injury – is the common experience of all living creatures. As an Opening Icebreaker, get people talking about their experiences of fear, particularly of those moments when someone came along and rescued them. How do we feel towards our rescuers?

The context of this last session is the siege of Jerusalem by the Assyrian army. God's people were in an impossible situation – surrender and be sent on a death march to Nineveh or resist and be starved out and slaughtered. Hezekiah chooses the only sensible option: he seeks the Lord. His prayer recognises the military reality but sees that ultimately this is a spiritual conflict. Do we serve the living God or do we serve man-made idols? Use Discussion Starter 2 to explore what this means for us in our present society.

There is a refreshing honesty in Hezekiah's prayer. Discussion Starter 3 asks us what we can learn from it. Note especially how Hezekiah is concerned for the glory of the Lord rather than simply for his own safety.

Read the Personal Application at this point. God always has a word for us when we seek Him with integrity. It is a word of deliverance. Use Discussion Starter 1 to consider together how the Lord rescues His people from evil. Your group members may come up with some inspiring examples from their own lives.

Food is crucial to a people under siege and facing the horrors of famine. God promises Hezekiah that He will lift the siege and there will be enough provision even though the invasion has prevented the land from being farmed. Indeed, in a short while his people will be cultivating the land and harvesting crops once again. What application does this have for us when we face uncertain economic times? Use Discussion Starter 5 to talk about divine provision.

Discussion Starter 4 provides us with an opportunity to discuss the role of angels in our lives. Invite testimonies but avoid speculation! In Isaiah's situation the Angel of the Lord destroys the Assyrian army overnight. Yet here the term almost certainly refers to a pre-incarnate manifestation of the warrior Christ. Read the Seeing Jesus section to help explain this. Note that the Lord does not underestimate the power and arrogance of sinful man organised against Him and His people. He deals justly and firmly with His enemies. Discussion Starter 7 encourages us to consider the lordship of Christ over the nations and the security that this should bring to the lives of His followers.

The coda to this section is Hezekiah's illness, prayer, miraculous recovery, and then his moment of folly. He showed the envoys from Babylon the full extent of his treasures. Was it vanity? Or an attempt to display the Lord's blessings? Either way, the Babylonian envoys simply made a shopping list. They would return, but next time with their army. Can we be guilty of similar folly? Use Discussion Starter 6 to explore the place of wisdom in our dealings with the world.

Isaiah's powerful prophecies are as relevant today as they ever were, and some have still to come to pass! The prophet is uncompromising in exposing evil but also absolutely and joyfully confident in the Lord's provision of a Saviour Messiah and of the ultimate triumph of justice over evil. It is a message to inspire us and to urge us on in our mission to spread the good news of Christ our Saviour. Encourage each member of your group to respond, 'Here am I. Send me!'

National Distributors

UK: (and countries not listed below)
CWR, Waverley Abbey House, Waverley Lane, Farnham, Surrey GU9 8EP.
Tel: (01252) 784700 Outside UK (44) 1252 784700

AUSTRALIA: CMC Australasia, PO Box 519, Belmont, Victoria 3216.
Tel: (03) 5241 3288 Fax: (03) 5241 3290

CANADA: David C Cook Distribution Canada, PO Box 98, 55 Woodslee Avenue, Paris, Ontario N3L 3E5.
Tel: 1800 263 2664

GHANA: Challenge Enterprises of Ghana, PO Box 5723, Accra.
Tel: (021) 222437/223249 Fax: (021) 226227

HONG KONG: Cross Communications Ltd, 1/F, 562A Nathan Road, Kowloon.
Tel: 2780 1188 Fax: 2770 6229

INDIA: Crystal Communications, 10-3-18/4/1, East Marredpalli, Secunderabad – 500026, Andhra Pradesh.
Tel/Fax: (040) 27737145

KENYA: Keswick Books and Gifts Ltd, PO Box 10242-00400, Nairobi.
Tel: (254) 20 312639/3870125

MALAYSIA: Salvation Book Centre (M) Sdn Bhd, 23 Jalan SS 2/64, 47300 Petaling Jaya, Selangor.
Tel: (03) 78766411/78766797   Fax: (03) 78757066/78756360

NEW ZEALAND: CMC Australasia, PO Box 303298, North Harbour, Auckland 0751.
Tel: 0800 449 408 Fax: 0800 449 049

NIGERIA: FBFM, Helen Baugh House, 96 St Finbarr's College Road, Akoka, Lagos.
Tel: (01) 7747429/4700218/825775/827264

PHILIPPINES: OMF Literature Inc, 776 Boni Avenue, Mandaluyong City.
Tel: (02) 531 2183 Fax: (02) 531 1960

SINGAPORE: Alby Commercial Enterprises Pte Ltd, 95 Kallang Avenue #04-00,
AIS Industrial Building, 339420.
Tel: (65) 629 27238 Fax: (65) 629 27235

SOUTH AFRICA: Struik Christian Books, 80 MacKenzie Street, PO Box 1144, Cape Town 8000.
Tel: (021) 462 4360 Fax: (021) 461 3612

SRI LANKA: Christombu Publications (Pvt) Ltd, Bartleet House, 65 Braybrooke Place, Colombo 2.
Tel: (9411) 2421073/2447665

TANZANIA: CLC Christian Book Centre, PO Box 1384, Mkwepu Street, Dar es Salaam.
Tel/Fax: (022) 2119439

USA: David C Cook Distribution Canada, PO Box 98, 55 Woodslee Avenue, Paris, Ontario N3L 3E5, Canada.
Tel: 1800 263 2664

For email addresses, visit the CWR website: www.cwr.org.uk

CWR is a registered charity – Number 294387

CWR is a limited company registered in England – Registration Number 1990308

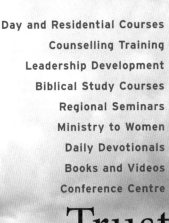

Trusted all Over the World

CWR HAS GAINED A WORLDWIDE reputation as a centre of excellence for Bible-based training and resources. From our headquarters at Waverley Abbey House, Farnham, England, we have been serving God's people for over 40 years with a vision to help apply God's Word to everyday life and relationships. The daily devotional *Every Day with Jesus* is read by nearly a million readers an issue in more than 150 countries, and our unique courses in biblical studies and pastoral care are respected all over the world. Waverley Abbey House provides a conference centre in a tranquil setting.

For free brochures on our seminars and courses, conference facilities, or a catalogue of CWR resources, please contact us at the following address:
CWR, Waverley Abbey House, Waverley Lane, Farnham, Surrey GU9 8EP, UK

Telephone: +44 (0)1252 784700
Email: mail@cwr.org.uk
Website: www.cwr.org.uk

 Applying God's Word
to everyday life and relationships

A DRAMATIC NEW RESOURCE

Esther is a piece of history that has it all: an orphaned girl from an ethnic minority becomes an empire's most powerful woman.

We have tears and intense sorrow, intrigue in high places, great joy and celebration – and what a line-up of colourful characters!

Esther: For such a time as this
by *Lynn Penson*
ISBN: 978-1-85345-511-7
Only **£3.99** (plus p&p)

Gain inspiration and insights as you enter the rich 'pantomime' that is the story of Esther.

Also available in the bestselling
Cover to Cover Bible Study Series

1 Corinthians
Growing a Spirit-filled church
ISBN: 978-1-85345-374-8

1 Timothy
Healthy churches – effective Christians
ISBN: 978-1-85345-291-8

23rd Psalm
The Lord is my shepherd
ISBN: 978-1-85345-449-3

2 Timothy and Titus
Vital Christianity
ISBN: 978-1-85345-338-0

Ecclesiastes
Hard questions and spiritual answers
ISBN: 978-1-85345-371-7

Ephesians
Claiming your inheritance
ISBN: 978-1-85345-229-1

Esther
For such a time as this
ISBN: 978-1-85345-511-7

Fruit of the Spirit
Growing more like Jesus
ISBN: 978-1-85345-375-5

Genesis 1–11
Foundations of reality
ISBN: 978-1-85345-404-2

God's Rescue Plan
Finding God's fingerprints on human history
ISBN: 978-1-85345-294-9

Great Prayers of the Bible
Applying them to our lives today
ISBN: 978-1-85345-253-6

Hebrews
Jesus – simply the best
ISBN: 978-1-85345-337-3

Hosea
The love that never fails
ISBN: 978-1-85345-290-1

Isaiah 1–39
Prophet to the nations
ISBN: 978-1-85345-510-0

James
Faith in action
ISBN: 978-1-85345-293-2

Jeremiah
The passionate prophet
ISBN: 978-1-85345-372-4

John's Gospel
Exploring the seven miraculous signs
ISBN: 978-1-85345-295-6

Joseph
The power of forgiveness and reconciliation
ISBN: 978-1-85345-252-9

Mark
Life as it is meant to be lived
ISBN: 978-1-85345-233-8

Moses
Face to face with God
ISBN: 978-1-85345-336-6

Nehemiah
Principles for life
ISBN: 978-1-85345-335-9

Parables
Communicating God on earth
ISBN: 978-1-85345-340-3

Philemon
From Slavery to Freedom
ISBN: 978-1-85345-453-0

Philippians
Living for the sake of the gospel
ISBN: 978-1-85345-421-9

Proverbs
Living a life of wisdom
ISBN: 978-1-85345-373-1

Revelation 1–3
Christ's call to the Church
ISBN: 978-1-85345-461-5

Revelation 4–22
The Lamb wins! Christ's final victory
ISBN: 978-1-85345-411-0

Rivers of Justice
Responding to God's call to righteousness today
ISBN: 978-1-85345-339-7

Ruth
Loving kindness in action
ISBN: 978-1-85345-231-4

The Covenants
*God's promises and their
relevance today*
ISBN: 978-1-85345-255-0

The Divine Blueprint
*God's extraordinary power in
ordinary lives*
ISBN: 978-1-85345-292-5

The Holy Spirit
Understanding and experiencing Him
ISBN: 978-1-85345-254-3

The Image of God
His attributes and character
ISBN: 978-1-85345-228-4

The Kingdom
Studies from Matthew's Gospel
ISBN: 978-1-85345-251-2

The Letter to the Colossians
In Christ alone
ISBN: 978-1-85345-405-9

The Letter to the Romans
Good news for everyone
ISBN: 978-1-85345-250-5

The Lord's Prayer
Praying Jesus' way
ISBN: 978-1-85345-460-8

The Prodigal Son
Amazing grace
ISBN: 978-1-85345-412-7

The Second Coming
Living in the light of Jesus' return
ISBN: 978-1-85345-422-6

The Sermon on the Mount
Life within the new covenant
ISBN: 978-1-85345-370-0

The Tabernacle
Entering into God's presence
ISBN: 978-1-85345-230-7

The Uniqueness of our Faith
What makes Christianity distinctive?
ISBN: 978-1-85345-232-1

£3.99 each (plus p&p)
Price correct at time of printing